*Joy Books II*

*To Mary Ann
God bless you.
Jane Parkyn*

# *Joy Books II*

## Jane E. Parkyn

iUniverse, Inc.
New York Lincoln Shanghai

# Joy Books II

Copyright © 2007 by Jane E. Parkyn

All rights reserved. No part of this book may be used or reproduced by any means, graphic, electronic, or mechanical, including photocopying, recording, taping or by any information storage retrieval system without the written permission of the publisher except in the case of brief quotations embodied in critical articles and reviews.

iUniverse books may be ordered through booksellers or by contacting:

iUniverse
2021 Pine Lake Road, Suite 100
Lincoln, NE 68512
www.iuniverse.com
1-800-Authors (1-800-288-4677)

Because of the dynamic nature of the Internet, any Web addresses or links contained in this book may have changed since publication and may no longer be valid.

The views expressed in this work are solely those of the author and do not necessarily reflect the views of the publisher, and the publisher hereby disclaims any responsibility for them.

ISBN: 978-0-595-43475-6 (pbk)
ISBN: 978-0-595-87802-4 (ebk)

Printed in the United States of America

Dedicated to all those who struggle to understand their feelings about themselves as well as others.

May your hearts be touched, your spirits strengthened, and the love of God fill you with His peace.

# *Contents*

| | |
|---|---|
| *Introduction* | *xiii* |
| Joy Books II | 1 |
| *Fall* | *3* |
| *Love* | *5* |
| *Seeds of Peace* | *7* |
| *Contentment* | *9* |
| *Evil* | *11* |
| *Words, Words* | *13* |
| *His Footsteps* | *15* |
| *My Prayer* | *17* |
| *He Cares* | *19* |
| *The Bridge of Life* | *21* |
| *Self* | *23* |
| *God's Calling* | *25* |
| *Defeat* | *27* |
| *God's Hand* | *29* |
| *Trouble* | *31* |
| *Your Job* | *33* |
| *Your Empty Space* | *35* |
| *A Plan for You* | *37* |
| *A Sinners Prayer* | *39* |
| *The Journey of Life* | *41* |

| | |
|---|---|
| Listening | 43 |
| Salt and Light | 45 |
| I Drew a Blank | 47 |
| Your Garden | 49 |
| Hope | 51 |
| To Do List | 53 |
| The Stranger | 55 |
| Good News | 57 |
| Time | 59 |
| Take the First Step | 61 |
| God's Warehouse | 63 |
| Love Toward Others | 65 |
| Know Thy Self | 67 |
| Who Am I | 69 |
| Waves | 71 |
| The Commander | 73 |
| The Marble Prisoners | 75 |
| The Love of Money | 77 |
| An Empty Place | 79 |
| Jesus Our Example | 81 |
| Well of Salvation | 83 |
| The Butterfly | 85 |
| God's Patchwork Quilt | 87 |
| Freedom | 89 |
| Your Mask | 91 |
| Where is the Christ Child | 93 |
| Guard Your Eyes | 95 |
| Be Silent | 97 |
| A Little Child | 99 |

| | |
|---|---|
| *His Blood* | *101* |
| *The Old House* | *103* |
| *Crucifixion* | *105* |
| *Christ Our Father* | *107* |
| *The Battle* | *109* |
| *The Homeless* | *111* |
| *The Tongue* | *113* |
| *United We Stand* | *115* |
| *From My Window* | *117* |
| *Turmoil* | *119* |
| *Downward Path* | *121* |
| *Traveling to Happiness* | *123* |
| *Your Reputation* | *125* |
| *The Aborted Child* | *127* |
| *Abortion—"A Mother's Loss"* | *129* |

# Acknowledgement

I've had many friends and family members encourage me in my writing.

My greatest fan and helper has been my dear husband, Billy. He has spent many hours placing my poetry on the computer as well as helping me organize my book. He is a loving, caring Christian man. Thank you sweetheart.

# Introduction

My writing first began when I wrote the eulogy for my brother, Jim, and then my daughter, Kimmie.

I've studied the Bible for many years and know what I write is inspired by God.

Being a nurse all my adult life, I've learned the importance of treating the whole person.(Mind, soul, and body)

All the experiences, good and bad, are what prepares us to help others in similar circumstances. Hopefully they teach us compassion, kindness, and love.

To focus on others, and not ourselves, takes discipline. This is not to say I've accomplished this challenge.

It can only be done by a daily walk with the Lord. Through prayer, we exercise our Faith. By studying God's word, we discover His grace.

*Joy Books II*

## *Enjoy the Moment*

I view the mountains and low lying fog in the valley and say, "Praise the Lord." How majestic it is.

The bare trees stand silhouetted against the sky like sentinels, but soon tiny buds will appear and a new season will begin. The natural wonder of it all tells of God's great creation. We experience seasons in our lives also. As young people, we want to hurry them along, and they seem to drag, but the older we get, the more quickly they pass.

Dear God, help us to enjoy the moment.

# *Fall*

Dry leaves are falling everywhere,
they flutter to the ground.
A magic carpet for our feet,
they never make a sound.

A rustling noise can be heard
as we walk a country lane,
to let us know that fall is here
and the season's begun to change.

A quiet starkness covers the land
as trees give up their leaves.
With bare and naked branches,
they stand silent before the freeze.

Our life is like the seasons,
a progression for us to make.
The plan conceived by God,
this journey we all must take.

## *Using Your Head*

The questions arise about our objectivity. Are we head strong and determined to have our own way? Can we step out of ourselves and look at the situation without bias or prejudice?

We have an on going battle with self. Pray to have an open mind and show consideration for others.

Love God with all your heart, soul and mind and love your neighbor as yourself.

## *Love*

Love is gentle and kind.
The flaws it doesn't see.
Compassion and understanding,
with love, comes easily.

Love is never envious.
It is loyal to the end.
It rejoices in the truth,
so let love be your friend.

Love is always forgiving.
Grudges shouldn't have a place.
It is a gift from God,
who saved us by His grace.

Be tender toward each person.
Allow for other's mistakes.
Let love be your companion
and let peace be what you make.

## *Peace*

Sowing peace is not easy, especially when you know you are right. We should ask ourselves, "What is right?" It can be different things to different people.

Being morally right as well as ethically right are something else. If what is happening is against God, then that's the time to take a stand. You may feel like the Lone Ranger, but remember to honor God in all things.

Ask the Holy Spirit's guidance.

# *Seeds of Peace*

May the seeds of peace
be the crop you sow.
May it be nourished with love
as you watch it grow.

May your harvest be rich
with many blessings for all.
May this bounty be shared
when the needy call.

May the fruit of the Spirit
grow in your soul.
May you plant seeds of goodness
to make others whole.

May you always be thankful.
May your harvest not cease
as you give praise to God
while you sow seeds of peace.

# *Prayer*

So many times in my life there was nothing I could do to solve a problem. Thinking that I was very self sufficient, I thought if I tried a little harder, I could fix it.

I can look back now and say, "Why didn't I let go and let God?"

We can wear ourselves out trying to do what only God can fix.

To grow in peace is a great gift from the Lord.

He is ABLE.

# *Contentment*

Learn the secret of contentment.
Focus on the meaning of life.
See the beauty all around you.
Give up your worry and strife.

Praise the Lord for your blessings.
Thank Him for the things He has done
to bring about the joy of living
in the race of life you run.

Guarantees will not be offered,
but His promises He will keep.
He'll give you strength for every day
to face the problems that you meet.

So be content and rest in God
and pray for peace within.
Remember He's your Heavenly Father
and you can always trust in Him.

# Evils of the World

In the world, many evils lurk. It is said in the Bible that we do not battle against flesh and blood, but against persons without bodies, evil rulers of the unseen world, mighty satanic beings.

This is a scary thought. I think of those unsaved people out there on their own.

When we don't walk with God, we are at the mercy of the world.

That doesn't mean we won't face challenges and problems, but we will have God to help us and strengthen us for battle.

# *Evil*

There's an evil in this world
that threatens your very soul.
It revels when you falter.
Destruction is his role.

He tries to get you unnerved
and destroy your belief.
He attacks you where you're weakest,
his goal to give you grief.

Don't give in to his goading,
for he enjoys your misery.
Take authority over him
to win the victory.

The word of God is your sword
to cut through his evil power.
A covering by the blood of the Lamb
will save you from being devoured.

Jesus is the answer for you.
Ask Him to live in your heart.
He says knock and the door will open
an never will He depart.

He is there to fight your battle.
Trust Him in all you do.
You will not be forsaken.
A protector He'll be for you.

## *Our Example*

Our example to others is not always what we say. Many times I would have been much better off as well as those around me, if I'd listened more and talked less.

A smile, showing courtesy in a parking lot, taking a back seat and leaving room for others etc, are a few examples.

The initials, "WWJD" (what would Jesus do) has become so popular that it warrants giving much thought to how we deal with problems and situations.

We must read His word to know Him.

# *Words, Words*

Words, words, how freely they flow.
Do they bless the audience?
Do we say more then we know?

Words, words, how they fall from our tongue.
Are they considerate of others?
Do they honor anyone?

Words, words, do we give much thought
how they effect those around us,
or what Jesus taught?

Words, words, do they make new friends?
Do we consider what we say
so there's nothing to mend?

May God's words always be our guide.
May we give love to others
from His presence deep inside.

# *Our Best Friend*

Looking back on my life, it seems I went through stages.

Depending on the stage, I would cultivate a good friend and then unfortunately as that stage dwindled, my friend and I seem to drift away from each other. I'm sure this is not true for all people.

It makes me think of the song, "What a Friend We Have in Jesus." He's always there. His love is unconditional and no matter what stage you are in life, He is there beside you, cheering you on.

## *His Footsteps*

Listen, do you hear them?
They're the footsteps of God.
They came before and now.
All over the world they trod.

Listen all about you.
His presence is always near.
Focus on the power of God.
Walk in His steps without fear.

Rise up in the morning
praising Him for the day.
Nourish yourself with His word.
It will help you find your way.

He will always carry you
when your heart is full of pain.
Listen for His footsteps.
Listen, He's calling your name.

# *Your Plan*

Did you ever wonder what God wanted you to do? I think about this often. Knowing the Lord has a plan for my life as well as yours, I still question which path to take.

Having faith to trust God is always a challenge, but we must rely on His promises. Jesus said in John 14:1, "Do not let your heart be troubled. Trust in God, trust also in Me".

## *My Prayer*

What is your will for me today, God?
What can I do to honor you?
Open my eyes that I can see
your presence in all I do.

Give me compassion like Jesus
and a heart that lives without fear.
Give me patience and understanding
for my loved ones that I hold dear.

Remind me that I must forgive
so I can dwell in the house of Lord.
Give me courage to witness for you
and help to remember your word.

Help me to love the unlovable
and pray for my enemies each day.
Give me good health and strength.
Motivate me to kneel and pray.

Thank you for listening, Father.
May blessings and love come to you.
I'll always love you, my Lord
for you're caring, loving and true.

## *Fear*

As a young child and on into my teens, I lived in fear of God. I'm not sure what I thought He would do. I just know I was afraid of Him.

There was never any affection shown in my family and I longed to hear someone say they loved me. I can look back now and see, however, that God always was there for me, and loved me.

How wonderful it would have been if I had only realized it.

## *He Cares*

As fear grips your heart with despair,
and you don't know which way to turn.
May God's tender mercy fill you
with love that can never be earned.

He's a gentle and caring Father
who reaches out with loving arms;
to be there when you need Him most;
to hold you and keep you from harm.

So lift up your burdens to Him.
Your sorrows He'll help you bear.
He loves you for the person you are
and wants you to know He cares.

## *Our Bridge*

God looked down through the centuries and saw that we would need a savior

He knew our weaknesses and wept, knowing His Son would have to be sacrificed for our sins. But He also knew that He would be raised from the dead to Glory.

Thanks be to God.

# *The Bridge of Life*

The bridge of life was planned
as God brooded over the mass.
Light appeared in dark places.
Day time and night were cast.

When creation was complete,
the Lord said it was good.
But Adam and Eve, His first children
didn't always do what they should.

The Lord looked down through the ages
and saw the corruption to come.
He knew a Bridge must be built
and it would be His sacrificed Son.

The Bridge was to save the world.
With a hammer and three nails it was made.
It was a safe place for crossing over.
His blood was the toll He paid.

In life, Jesus Christ is your Bridge.
His robe of righteousness awaits you.
Drape yourself in its salvation
and wear it in all that you do.

# *Giving*

To give up self seeking and focus on the needs of others is what Jesus calls us to do.

How easy it is to get caught up in self and how boring this way of thinking can be.

The happiest times are when we are giving.

We should pray for a generous spirit, one that delights in giving.

May the spirit of Christmas reign in our hearts daily.

# *Self*

Self gathers up its listeners,
his performance he knows so well.
He spends much time rehearsing
the stories he likes to tell.

With self, he's usually not bored
but sometimes does get down.
Self needs to have an audience
to whom he can expound.

He doesn't listen to others,
for what he has to say,
is more important than listening
to the happenings of the day.

If self is trying to consume you,
take authority over him.
Be a careful listener
and let self stay within.

## *Our Focus*

The busyness of our lives hinders our focus. This we can attribute to the demands of other people, but in reality it is the path we've chosen to trod.

We need to regroup and get our priorities straight. A too busy mind can miss God's calling.

Attentive listening is a gift. We must find time to commune with God. Put Him first and abide in His presence

# God's Calling

Some ride the waves of life,
denying the existence of God.
When the storms pound on their shore,
do they look at the road they've trod?

When anxious moments arise,
where do they search for peace?
Is it in another success
or worldliness to find relief?

They wander over the land,
like nomads searching for rest.
They pitch their tents with others
looking for happiness.

How foolish is their pursuit.
Contentment is at their door.
In God they should place their trust.
He beckons them from the shore.

## Missing the Mark

All my adult life I've pressured myself into hitting the mark and would replay, in my mind, all the misses. I tended to think God was keeping score.

    I still find myself falling into that trap.

    I must remind myself that my life is a gift from God and He wants me to be filled with joy. God wants this for all His children.

    Sorrows will come, but He's always there to weep with us.

## *Defeat*

I stand on the threshold of defeat
while success is passing me by.
I cry to the Lord for help
but I can't hear his reply.

Humiliation clouds my thinking
as I deal with my wounded pride.
I want to run from the players
and find a place to hide.

My soul hungers for success
while others laugh and have fun.
Help me Lord, to be a good loser
and not to turn and run.

Thank you for my lesson on defeat
and being with me through the pain.
I know it's not if you win or lose,
but how you play the game.

## Why Me

Suffering builds character, it is said. My response is, "Stop Lord, I think I've had enough."

Over the years, as I faced problems, I remember crying out to the Lord, "Why me?"

Hind sight being 20/20, I can say now, "Why not me." Compared to some people, my problems were miniscule.

During a stressful situation, is when I felt closest to God.

It's too bad that it took problems to draw Him close.

# God's Hand

The unseen hand of God
moves over the world with ease,
looking for those in need,
and His children He wishes to please

His creating never ends.
His healing continues on.
Laughter blesses Him.
His truth, a place to rest upon.

Our God stays at His watch
even when we are asleep.
He promises He'll never leave us.
Our souls, He will always keep.

Trust Him with your problems.
Talk to Him in prayer.
Rest in His tender love,
for His Spirit is everywhere.

## *Trust and Obey*

The words of an old song, trust and obey, seem to get lost in our anxieties.

As we struggle with a problem, we finally decide to place it on the altar of God. The unfortunate part about this is, we go back and pick it up again.

Trusting God is like boarding a plane and trusting the pilot to get us to our destination.

When there's something bothering us that we absolutely can't resolve, we must pray and trust our Father to take care of it.

# *Trouble*

Trouble knocks on your door.
He wants to attack your mind.
His hunger is never satisfied.
He can arrive just anytime.

Clever and cunning is he
as he silently stalks his prey.
He watches your every move
while following you throughout the day.

When trouble is all around you
and you don't know which way to turn,
send praises and love to our Father
and get mercy in return.

His light will always guide you
and joy will fill your heart.
Though trouble may try your patience,
God will never depart.

# *Your Job*

There is a saying, "He who considers his work beneath him will be above doing it well."

Once a foreign ambassador came to the United States to represent his country. After getting off the plane, he went to the restroom. His escorts waited and waited and finally went to check on him. They found him just finishing up cleaning the sinks and picking up papers.

Any job is honorable and should be done well.

May what we do and say honor God.

# *Your Job*

The whistle blows at seven
calling workmen to their job.
Some are full of vim and vigor,
others just dragging along.

The time clock stands waiting
and each one takes his turn.
Some with cheerful chatter.
Some counting what they'll earn.

They hurry to their position
and start to work away.
Some are laughing with joy.
Some anxious for the end of the day.

Again the whistle blows
and the workday comes to an end.
Some are rushing to the time clock
while others visit with a friend.

When you hear the whistle blowing,
how do you start your day?
Do you face it with laughter and joy
or are you already counting your pay?

## *Success Through Filling Your Empty Space*

It has been said that success is not the position you reach in life, but the obstacles you overcome.

In a speech by Jack Eckerd, the drug store magnate, he said that though very successful, he never found peace until he totally turned his life over to Christ.

In Punta Gorda, Florida where I lived more than forty years, I remember seeing Mr. Eckerd hobbling around his store with a cast on his leg. He earned his success.

If there's a space that needs filled in you, try Jesus. He is waiting on your call.

## *Your Empty Space*

You wonder what it is
this empty space within.
The worldly things don't seem to help.
How can its filling begin?

Will you help me, God, to understand?
Will you help me fill this space?
"Of course I will", the Lord replied.
"It's called my Holy Place."

"Honor me in all you do
and help your fellowman.
I'll help you fill this empty space,
and will reveal to you, my plan."

## *God's Plan*

The Lord hears your prayer. He made you. He was there while you were being formed in your mother's womb.

God planned everyday of your life. He is the Alpha and the Omega. (the beginning and the end)

He loved you so much that He sent His only Son to die for your sins.

You have a place reserved in Heaven if you will turn your life over to Jesus Christ.

Thanks be to God.

# *A Plan for You*

God knows the plan He has for you.
Fear not and walk in peace.
Let your heart be full of hope
and your stress will be released.

Though pain and suffering come your way,
God will see you through.
He's a loving, tender Father
and cares what happens to you.

He says, "Pray and seek Me in earnest."
A good future will be your reward.
Praise Him for His goodness
for He has much for you in store.

He knows when a sparrow falls.
On your head, He numbers each hair.
Give your troubles to the Lord.
He will lift you out of despair.

Jeremiah 29:11; Luke 12:6-7

## *Forgiven*

When we pray and repent of our sins, we've been washed by the blood of the lamb.

Our problem is we can't forget our sins. We keep going back to God asking Him to forgive us for sins that He has already forgiven.

We must have faith that they are long forgotten by our Father, and not keep plowing the same field over and over again.

Forgive us Lord.

# *A Sinners Prayer*

Overlook my youthful sin.
Please make my record clean.
Correct me when I'm wrong.
Your forgiveness, help me glean.

May your eyes be full of mercy
as you teach me to obey.
Let the fragrance of your love
keep me from going astray.

Surround me with your blessings.
Let my pardoned soul be free.
Save me from my troubles.
May your goodness follow me.

Help me sing your praises
and live in your presence each day.
May I delight in your glory
and hear you, Lord, as I pray.

# *Happiness*

Planting and hoeing may not be fun, but the harvest awaits.

It is hard to measure happiness. As a child it might be a birthday party or as a teenager, dancing with the person you pined over for months. To the farmer, it can be an abundant harvest.

Happiness seems to me a time of striving to accomplish something and yet in the end it's remembered only for a short time.

May your journey in life be filled with happiness and contentment.

# *The Journey of Life*

We enter this world on a journey,
with no road map to show us the way.
We're at the mercy of our keepers,
to care for us thru the day.

We soon can walk about
and our environment takes its hold.
We develop into a person.
Thoughts come from what we are told.

We wonder about our self
and think of things we've done.
Our environment is our dictator
for what we may become.

There's a struggle to overcome
the dark places in our life.
We deal with outside pressure
and live in this world of strife.

Happiness may be fleeting
but its presence can have great worth,
if we take this journey of life
and find God in our daily search.

# *A Full Life*

As I'm living a full life, the years are flying by so quickly. I strive to do God's will but neglect to ask Him what it is at times.

I tend to be a Martha instead of a Mary. Martha was always busy preparing and doing while Mary sat at the feet of Jesus.

What we really need is balance. Too much striving doesn't allow enough time for listening.

My prayer is, "God, help me to listen to what I'm hearing."

# *Listening*

We hear but do not listen
to what others have to say.
Their words seem only words
with nothing to relay.

We drift into self centered thought
and plan our anxious reply.
Not listening to what's being said,
"I'm important," is our cry.

Stop and focus on the sender.
Look him in the eye.
Listen to what he's saying
and make a thoughtful reply.

Care about this person.
Touch him with your heart.
Give your undivided attention
and smile when you depart.

## Be the Seasoning

People hunger for encouragement. With the pressures that exist in our lives today, we long for understanding and love.

A pat on the back goes a long way. It can be one of the best gifts you can give someone.

Be the seasoning in a world that is losing its flavor.

# *Salt and Light*

Seek to be the seasoning
like salt is to your food.
Give flavor to the world
by what you say and do.

If seasoning's lost its flavor,
of what value can it be?
When Christians show no love,
what effect will others see?

When we walk in darkness
not showing others Christ's Light,
how will their eyes be opened?
How will they know what He's like?

Our light is being hidden
when we're quiet and don't speak
or by going along with the crowd
when it's God that we should seek.

May we be the salt and the light
with flavor and with glow.
Let's be beacons for the Lord
and witness wherever we go.

Matthew 5:13-16

## *An Embarrassing Time*

Did you ever have to give a speech as a kid, perform in a play, or sing a solo, and your mind went totally blank? What a sick, sinking feeling that is.

I always had a hard time forgiving myself when I made some faux pas or drew a total blank when performing or talking.

God doesn't want us to beat ourselves up over incidentals. There is so much sadness and despair in the world, that the little things are insignificant.

## *I Drew a Blank*

I drew a blank then panicked
and stared out over the crowd.
The blush of embarrassment covered me,
as the silence grew very loud.

I listened for prompting to come
but the dead silence prevailed.
The crowd stirred in their seats
as my conscience shouted, "You failed."

Where's there a place to hide?
I just want to escape and run.
Despair filled my heart
as I mourned what I had done.

Suddenly my mine was clear.
God came and rescued me.
He must have heard my prayer
for He answered my frantic plea.

With courage, I started again
and peace drifted over the crowd.
Applause rose up to Heaven
and God looked down and smiled.

# The Garden

Being involved in gardening for years, I'm well aware of the ravages of neglect. Weeds can take over and leach nourishment from your plantings. Your harvest will be scant and lack quality.

It's the same with our soul. When starved for the word of God, it will struggle to produce good fruit.

Dear God, help us to always tend the gardens of our soul well.

# *Your Garden*

There's a garden in your soul
that needs tending every day.
Plant seeds of love and kindness
to feed you on your way.

Water it with the word of God,
for self-righteousness and greed
will come to over power it
and take over like a weed.

Let the seeds of compassion
grow strong with tender care.
Give them nourishment from Heaven,
for we know our Lord is there.

Bless others from your garden.
Harvest the best for the Lord.
Let love be your goal
and joy will be your reward.

## Problems in Life

How painful it is to watch our children or friends struggle with problems in life.

Most of the time there is not a whole lot we can do to help fix things, but we can pray and be a good listener.

We can all be encouragers and instill hope.

Despair is so painful. We have all been there at one time or another in our lives.

Plant seeds of hope through the help of God.

## *Hope*

I look through the window of despair
and pray for a reason to hope.
An overwhelming sadness fills me,
a sorrow worn like a cloak.

I wonder about tomorrow.
Will it bring this sorrow relief?
Where will I go to find help?
How long will I carry this grief?

God, if you are there, please help me.
Save me from all this pain.
A longing peace,I covet,
my hope for tomorrow regain.

My spirit is suddenly quiet.
A loving presence is there.
This reminder from my Lord,
that I'll always be in His care.

## *My Agenda*

How I struggle to discipline myself and follow my own schedule.

Here it is a new year and I plan to exercise, write, learn to draw, and the list goes on and on. Well, needless to say, I'm slowly not fulfilling my agenda.

I'm learning that I should only try to carry out my plans for one day. Looking too far ahead is defeating.

God reminds me that I should let tomorrow take care of itself.

Long term goals are fine if we don't let them become burdens.

## *To Do List*

There's a list that grows daily,
a reminder of things to do.
It covers many pages,
these projects, we don't seem to get to.

The minutes of the day tick by
and we say, "We'll catch up tomorrow."
Our To Do List, gets longer and longer
with unfinished tasks, our sorrow.

On this treadmill of life we march
while God watches for His cue.
He patiently waits in the wings
as we scan our list of things to do.

With months and years drifting by,
in the shuffle, our list gets lost.
As we strive to stay focused,
our pursuance, we exhaust.

"What is the answer?" we ask.
Will this To Do List never end?
God lovingly smiles and whispers,
I'll help you and be your friend.

# *The Poor Tattered Man*

What is our approach to a poor disheveled person who happens into our lives?

A preacher once disguised himself as a poor tattered man and entered the church. Nobody came up to him and greeted him. He could hear whispers from the parishioners. There was a wave of discomfort around him.

The preacher then went up to the pulpit, removed his disguise and made himself known to the congregation.

He said, "That was your sermon for the day.

He then turned and walked off the platform.

# *The Stranger*

The church was filled with people
reaching for a friendly hand,
when suddenly silence fell.
At the door, stood a poor tattered man.

He looked very gaunt and weary
as he stood quietly at the door.
He limped slowly up the aisle
and then sat down on the floor.

The people looked at each other,
wide eyed, with eyebrows raised.
Whispers were heard all around.
At the poor tattered man, they gazed.

Then an old elder of the church
stood up and walked toward the man.
He smiled and greeted him
and reached for the strangers hand.

They sat together on the floor
with tears streaming down their face.
They stared at the old rugged cross
feeling the love and blessing of God's grace.

# *The Good News*

The Good News doesn't make headlines. For the most part, it's not well known around the world.

In God's word we are pledged to tell the Good News to all we meet. It's sad to say, but usually this is something we shy away from.

What better News could we pass on, than that Jesus Christ is the truth, the light and the way, and that He came to save our souls.

# Good News

Jesus wants to be our Lord.
From Heaven, is where He came.
In a common manger born,
yet there was power in His name.

Temptations were always before Him
as He waxed strong in body and mind.
He chose the narrow road
as a servant to all mankind.

Though mocked by the world,
He prayed forgiveness for their souls.
He pleaded with the Father
for their hearts to be made full.

Jesus carried the Old Rugged Cross
so He could die for His chosen ones.
He was pierced for our sins
while His Father wept for His Son.

How the angels sang from Heaven
as Jesus rose to the Father above.
The Comforter, the Holy Spirit,
is a reminder of His love.

# *Time*

One of the news reels I saw as a kid said, "Time Marches On." We only realize this as we get older.

The first question Jesus will ask when we get to Heaven is, "What did you do with your life?" I just hope I have a good answer.

There's a saying, it's not how many hours you put in, but how much you put into the hours.

My prayer is, "Lord, please help me to be a good steward of my time."

# *Time*

Time continues its relentless march,
never stopping for rest.
Favorites, it doesn't have
so always struggle to do your best.

When anxious moments are overwhelming,
time seems to drag its feet.
You watch minutes tick slowly by
with no one shouting, "Retreat."

When good times give birth to joy,
you hope it will never end.
Time marches by too quickly
when you have fences to mend.

Precious moments can be gone forever
leaving thoughts filled with regret.
When time has passed you by,
sorrow can be what is left.

So let time always be your friend.
Honor it as you honor the Lord.
Lost time cannot be recaptured
and doesn't hold any reward.

## *Procrastination*

Do you find yourself saying, "I'll put it off until tomorrow." Unfortunately tomorrow doesn't always come. We all procrastinate.

Someone once said, "It takes more to plow a field than merely turning it over in our mind."

The road to failure is paved with good intentions.

The question we must ask ourselves is, "What fields are waiting for us to plow?'

All that God created was done with order giving us a perfect example of how to live our lives.

## *Take the First Step*

There's much for me to do.
Tell me, Lord, where to begin.
Questions real in my mind
as turmoil boils within.

Project after project awaits
as I sit and stare into space.
I must stand and take the first step
if I'm going to win this race.

Then I hear the voice of God,
"Take courage and face the day.
Praise me for the answers
you'll receive as you kneel and pray."

I smile and take my first step
for I know God's in control.
With thankful heart I march on.
His presence has made me whole.

## *Suffering Builds Character*

Throughout my life I tried to fix everything; a broken heart, a broken life due to alcohol, sickness, sadness etc.

It has taken me years to mature enough to realize I can't fix everything.

My job is to be loving, kind, and understanding.

God doesn't fix everything. In His wisdom, He allows us to struggle at times with our problems.

It's not that He doesn't love us, but it's because He loves so much, and wants us to turn to Him.

Suffering builds character.

# God's Warehouse

There's a warehouse up in heaven
stocked with answers to prayer.
It's filled to overflowing
with parts to make repairs.

Each shelf has something special,
just what we might need
to fix a broken promise
or a reward for a good deed.

This resource is not always tapped
though its replies are always free.
We blindly search for resolve
but the answers we do not see.

When troubles seem to surround us
and we don't know what to do,
God's warehouse stands there waiting
saying, "Pray, I have help for you."

# *A Generous Heart*

It is said in Proverbs 11:25 that a generous soul will be made rich, and he who waters will also be watered himself.

Treat others like you want to be treated. Show mercy always and give as though giving to the Lord.

Pray to God for a generous and kind heart. These gifts He will gladly give.

## *Love Toward Others*

Be gentle and kind to others
and always ready to forgive.
Grudges that are carried
will affect the way you live.

Show tenderhearted mercy
and be patient while you wait.
God knows our every thought
so don't let love turn to hate.

Do what you know is right
though condemned by the world around.
Give up any evil desires.
Let the teachings of Christ abound.

Pray for your enemy each day.
Reach out to those in need.
"What you do for others," says God,
"You do it unto me."

## *Let Go and Let God*

I just read this statement that should lift anyone's anxiety.

Quote: "I've suffered a great many catastrophes in my life. Most of them never happened."

Quite profound, isn't it?

How we worry about insignificant things that never come to fruition. 1 Peter 5:7 says, "Let Him have all your worries and cares, for He is always thinking about you and watching everything that concerns you."

We need to let go and let God.

## *Know Thy Self*

Our trials are a testing ground,
adversity, our teacher each day.
They help us face tomorrow.
For them, we should stand and praise.

Who we are is where we've been
and troubles that vexed our soul.
They helped us with our challenges
as we've played out our life's role.

When looking back on yesterdays,
when did the Lord seem close?
Was it when all was going well
that you needed Him the most?

Wasn't it in the bad times
you asked God to meet your need?
Those anxious times were blessings,
this fact you must concede.

So praise God in the worst times
as well as the good times too.
He will sooth your troubled soul.
His love will comfort you.

# Wisdom

In Proverbs 4, it says "Learn to be wise. Cling to wisdom—she will protect you. Love her—she will guard you."

Wisdom can be passed on from generation to generation.

We have a promise from God that if we seek wisdom from Him, we will have a long happy life.

Seeking wisdom is one of the most important things we can do.

Pray for wisdom.

# *Who Am I*

I existed long ago
before the world began.
I watched as springs bubbled forth
spilling over dry land.

My strength causes kings to reign.
Unending riches I give.
My paths of justice and right
teach people how to live.

I love those who love me
and show them common sense.
My advice is always good.
Understanding, I dispense.

When God made His blueprint,
I was at His side.
I rejoiced at all creation.
In Him, I abide.

      Wisdom.

# *Waves*

It is hard to realize how a person could watch the waves wash up on shore and not believe in the Great Creator God.

His laws of nature speak volumes. There is no way that all creation just evolved.

We see much, but do we really look closely at what we're seeing? The tiniest perfect flower is a sample of His Godly touch.

Look closely at what you see.

## *Waves*

The waves come pounding on the shore.
Their cadence continues unchanged.
A frothy foam spreads over the sand,
then washes back out again.

This rhythm's held by a steady hand
and never loses its beat.
A crescendo comes with a booming crash,
but the cadence doesn't retreat.

The steady hand of the Conductor
moves over the sea with ease.
Our God directs this symphony
for His audience He wishes to please.

## Who We Are in Christ

How sad it is that so many in our world don't know the saving grace of Christ. We all have problems with which we must deal.

God never said life would be easy. For those in Christ, there is someone to help carry their heavy load.

Place your burdens at the foot of the cross and be saved by His grace.

# *The Commander*

The commander of the Heavenly Army
gives orders to stand firm.
He's come to save His children
and bring ruin to the enemy in turn.

Let the people clap with joy
and hail the King of Kings,
for He is a mighty Father
and creator of everything.

Shout praises to the Lord.
Thank Him for blessing you.
Let trumpets' blasts greet Him,
for He's coming to our rescue.

May honors come from nations.
May everyone bow down,
for the Commander of the Heavenly Armies
came and set aside His crown.

He sacrificed Himself
and took on all our sin.
Though He was Lord of all,
they mocked and crucified Him.

His sacrifice was His choice
to which we should applaud,
for our Lord Jesus Christ
was also our Creator God.

## *God's Plan for You*

God knew you before you were conceived and saw you while you were being formed in your mother's womb.

He planned each day of your life. That doesn't mean we're like robots. We do have choices.

God wants us to choose Him. He will help you make Godly decisions and walk the path laid out for you.

# *The Marble Prisoners*

Michelangelo saw the prisoners
entombed in a marble wall.
He raised his hammer and chisel,
for he could hear them call.

Like David, they shouted to be free.
In a dungeon of silence, they lived.
Through the master's vision released,
this gift to the world, he'd give.

Like the master, God saw you
incased in your mothers womb.
Our great sculpture, God,
knew you would be arriving soon.

Your future was already planned
but your choice, He freely gave.
His word would give you direction.
Through His Son, you would be saved.

The painful suffering and problems
were the tools the Father used.
He allowed them to chisel the character
that would only belong to you.

# *The Love of Money*

How sad it is to see greedy people oppress the poor. We hear more and more of large company executives stealing from their own employees. Their arrogance makes us wonder how they could blatantly pad their own pockets.

Jesus taught that you can't serve both God and money. We can only have one master.

All we have belongs to God. Of the 100% He gives us, He only asks for 10% in return.

# *The Love of Money*

Where do you place your trust?
Is it in money or worldly things?
Do you covet your neighbor's possessions
and think what happiness they'd bring?

What occupies your mind?
What is your foremost thought?
Is your focus on your blessings
and what our Father taught?

Money can be the root of all evil
if love of it,is your goal.
There's a price you will pay
that will take a heavy toll.

Good stewards we're to be,
with His wisdom being our guide.
A plentiful harvest will come
if we give God His tithe.

## *Her Space*

My daughter died at age 41. The pain of her loss lingers on. The space she occupied in my heart continues. Nothing can fill her space.

I am comforted by the Holy Spirits presence, but I still mourn my loss.

I praise the Lord I will be with her someday along with my other loved ones who have gone before me.

## *An Empty Place*

Over an empty place I mourn
which time cannot fill.
Memories of my lost loved one,
battles with God's will.

Busyness can bring escape
but the empty place lingers on.
My longing heart weeps
for my loved one who is gone.

We stand in line for our turn
to form an empty space.
Will what we do be remembered
or will another take our place?

Now is the hour to plan
before your journey is through.
Now is the time to pray
and ask God what you're to do.

He's waiting for your knock at the door
to give you direction for life.
Step out of that long line
and listen to our Lord's advice.

# Faith of a Child

Jesus is so full of love. All creation is filled with His presence.

When the disciples told the mothers with their babies to go away, Jesus said "Let the little children come unto me." He tenderly blessed them and said that in order for anyone to get in the kingdom's gates, he must have the faith of a little child.

Pray for God to strengthen your faith.

# Jesus Our Example

He walked along a dusty road
with children scrambling for His hand.
Song birds flew from branch to branch
singing to the Great I Am.

Baby animals jumped and played
giving pleasure to our Lord.
He sprinkled nature with His joy
so we would never be bored.

As we walk our life's road,
flowers beckon us on the way.
"Stop and enjoy our fragrance,"
is what they seem to say.

Have our lives become too busy?
Do we hurry and walk on by?
Do we take all creation for granted?
Are we annoyed by a baby's cry?

Let's take the hand of Jesus
as we walk along life's road.
Let's love and bless our neighbor
and help carry his heavy load.

## *Standing Firm*

There is much pollution in this world—not only chemicals, but evil persons spreading their wickedness. Saddam Hussein was a prime example. He killed his own citizens and even family members.

Though evil seems to be running rampant, God's people are standing firm.

Give us courage Lord, to honor you in what we say, do and think.

May your well of salvation never go dry.

# *Well of Salvation*

There's a Heavenly flowing well
whose water is pure and clear.
This Godly place will quench your thirst
and drive away your fear.

Many have drunk from this well
yet others walk on by.
With thoughts of a worldly well,
the saving waters they deny.

The wells of the world are polluted
with poisons ending in death.
God's Holy well runs clear
for His is the very best.

Ask, for His water is free.
From His well, blessings will pour.
Drink from His well of salvation
and you won't thirst anymore.

## *Our Purpose*

We do not have to be alone in our struggles. Jesus is waiting for each of us to accept Him.

The butterfly must struggle to escape from the cocoon or he will not survive.

We can survive in Christ. How wonderful is God's creation. He has purpose in all that He does.

We should pray for wisdom to understand His plan for each of us.

# *The Butterfly*

There's darkness all about him,
like a soul without the Lord.
A promised resurrection
will come by God's spoken word.

The butterfly works and struggles
within his tomb to be free.
This he must do all alone
as Christ did on that tree.

Like the butterfly's resurrection,
the dead in Christ are saved.
A new body will embrace them
as they're lifted from the grave.

May the butterfly remind you,
when you see his wings at rest,
like folded hands to God,
to give thanks for all He's blessed.

## *America*

America is such a unique country. The pilgrims came searching for freedom. Since then, thousands have come to our shores.

Our country reminds me of a patchwork quilt with patches sown together to make one large quilt. Though different, they all seem to blend.

God bless America.

# God's Patchwork Quilt

God gathers up the pieces
with contrast as His goal.
He uses many textures
in His quilt to make it whole.

The pieces are placed together
according to His plan.
His sewing is sometimes painful,
this quilt from the Great I Am.

It's made of many colors
but they all seem to blend,
for this quilt is all the people
He gathers up to mend.

God knew we needed contrast
to add beauty to our life,
from people of many colors
to make His quilt just right.

## *Let Freedom Ring*

Because of terrorist's attacks on America, our country suffers from unrest. We took our freedom for granted. Now we tend to be more suspect. We wonder what is in the offing. May our bell of freedom ring again.

"God bless America," has become our standard bearer. As it is sung throughout the land, we feel united in the Lord

Thanks be to God.

## *Freedom*

Near the shore stands Ms. Liberty,
her lamp lifted on high.
A guide for wandering souls,
with freedom being their cry.

Battles were fought for this freedom
with millions of lives lost.
The greedy war-lords of this world
didn't bother to count the cost.

America is the land of the free
where immigrants flood to her shore.
May they be greeted with open arms
and not have to wander any more.

A price was paid for this freedom
by our loved ones called to serve.
Some gave their lives as a sacrifice,
a death they didn't deserve.

Let's always honor the brave
and remember the price they paid.
Praise God for our freedom
and His protection every day.

## The Masks We Wear

How pretentious we can be. We mask our feelings and make excuses.

What are these, other than white lies? I don't know where the term white lie came from, but it seems to me that a lie is a lie.

It's like stealing a nickel or a hundred dollar bill. It is still stealing.

Making an excuse is just a way we lie to cover our irresponsibility.

If I'm pointing my finger at you, I have three more pointing back at myself.

We all fall short of the glory of God.

# Your Mask

The masks that we wear
are held firm in place.
They can be a deceiving glance,
as they disguise our face.

There's a mask that covers pride
when hurt feelings reign.
Another hides self righteousness
while judging others pain.

We wear a mask of excuses
for things we haven't done.
We give them little thought
as they roll off our tongue.

These masks can be removed
if we change what's inside.
Through God's gracious forgiveness,
we'll have nothing left to hide.

## *The Spirit of Giving*

Though Christmas may seem far removed, the spirit of Christmas should live within us daily.

The spirit of Christmas is the spirit of the Living, Giving God.

What a blessing it is to give. The giver, more times than not, is blessed more than the receiver.

What fun it can be to buy something special for someone you love or reach out and give your time and money to a needy cause.

Celebrate Christmas daily.

# Where is the Christ Child

Where is the joy of Christmas
with its tinsel and evergreen tree?
Where did we leave the Christ Child?
Christmas Spirit, where can He be?

It's only a short time passed
when children gazed in awe
at presents piled on high
and could hardly believe all they saw.

How quickly we soon forget
when decorations are taken down.
As the spirit of Christmas fades,
the Christ Child cannot be found.

The gifts are lost in the shuffle.
Our dailiness, we try to regain.
Where did we lose the Christ Child?
In our hearts, He should've remained.

Next year we'll try to do better.
Less hurried, is what we say.
Where did we lose the Christ Child
in our busyness of the day?

# The Worldly Evils

It has come more and more to our attention that seeing violence on TV has stimulated violent acts in some people.

Parents are cautioned to monitor what their children watch or read. Many schools must use metal detectors to spot weapons being carried by pupils.

Terrorism has invaded our country. Though evil seems all around us, we must not walk in fear.

Remember God is still in control. Pray for His love and protection daily.

# *Guard Your Eyes*

Guard your eyes of what you see.
Run from all worldly sin.
There's evil all around you,
waiting to suck you in.

The spirit world lurks in shadows
looking for those to devour.
It attacks you where you're weakest
to destroy you with its power.

These spirits are fallen angles
that wanted to be like God.
They were thrown down from Heaven,
for their evil didn't belong.

Keep your eyes focused on God.
Fill your heart with His love.
Turn your life over to Him
so you'll be covered by His blood.

# *Prayer*

Most of the time when praying, I'm talking away and not keeping silent before the Lord. How can I expect to hear from Him if I don't listen?

Did you ever stop to think how patient God must be?

He knows us so well and what we need. We must read His word and listen as He speaks to our heart.

## *Be Silent*

Regret not your silence,
when a spoken word would sting.
Have a contrite heart.
Be charitable in everything.

Let your spoken word be reverent
toward God and those who hear.
May you always abide in the Father.
Let Him be the one you revere.

Keep silent before the Lord.
Use judgment in what you say.
Give credence to His Holy Word.
It's Him you should obey.

The Lord will be coming soon.
Repent for the wrongs you've done.
Sing praises to His name
as you give honor to the Holy One.

## A Child

I hope not one of us will ever take a little child for granted, and not realize what a precious gift they are from God.

It is sad to think of the child abuse that seems to be more and more prevalent.

I pray that we will be alert to any sign of abuse.

God, bless the children of this world.

# A Little Child

A little child is a gift from God,
his innocence a joy to behold.
He sees no wrong in those around
and usually does what he is told.

His imagination soars to the sky
as he rides his heavenly train.
He jumps with joy as the whistle blows,
his jubilance without restrain.

Quiet down, he's sometimes told
by his charges for the day.
There's no train up in the sky.
"You're much too noisy," they say.

"But I saw my train as it whistled by,"
says the tiny little child.
"I only want to ride on it,"
looking up with a great big smile.

His charges frown and walk away.
This child they don't understand.
"I will ride his heavenly train,"
says God, as He takes his hand.

## Christ's Sacrifice

It is hard to comprehend the cross. Jesus agonized when praying before His crucifixion, for He knew the worst part would be His separation from the Father. Our sins on Christ were what caused the separation.

I pray God will help each of us to understand His unending love.

# *His Blood*

In agony Jesus knelt down
for His time was coming soon.
On the cross to be separated from the Father,
would be His most painful wound.

As Jesus prayed to God,
His sweat was like drops of blood.
His tortured spirit cried out
to the weeping Father above.

Jesus prayed for the horror to be removed,
but He said, "I want your will, not mine."
A mission that must be accomplished
for the salvation of all mankind.

The Lord sent a heavenly angel
to minister to Jesus that day.
Strength was given to Him
as He knelt before the Father to pray.

Jesus journeyed on to the cross.
In a borrowed tomb He was laid.
The precious blood of the Lamb
was the sacrifice that was made.

# The Past

Driving through the mountains of beautiful North Carolina, where I live, I'd see an abandoned farmhouse sometimes. It makes me wonder about those that lived there and the children that once played in the yard.

There is such a thing called "The law of Entropy." If neglected overtime, things lose energy, decay and move from order to disorder.

If we neglect our body, mind and spirit and not walk with God, our body (the house where God lives) will become spent just like the old farmhouse.

## *The Old House*

The old house stands in silence.
Her tin roof worn with rust.
The porch swing sways gently
while a cold wind blows the dust.

Wild vines wrap arms about her,
like a mother cradling her child.
The old house stands deserted,
surrounded by plantings gone wild.

Shutters bang in the wind.
The door hinge cries for oil.
I wonder where the children are
and their parents who sweated and toiled?

This house with its quiet continence,
a monument made to last,
stands with weeping memories
of good times from the past.

There's a sadness that fills my heart,
seeing the old dilapidated home.
I think of all its yesterdays
as it stands here all alone.

I'm reminded of where I live,
to keep it happy and in repair
so God the Master Builder
is made welcome and able to live there.

## The Cross

We humans are unable to comprehend the cross. The physical pain that Jesus endured must have been excruciating. But worse than the physical pain was the pain of being separated from the Father. God could not look upon His Son while He carried our sins.

We are saved by the shed blood of the Lamb, Jesus.

## *Crucifixion*

Oh Father, I think of your pain
as you hung on the cross for me.
My eyes fill with tears of sorrow.
How alone you were on that tree.

Your Mother knelt there and cried
wondering why this torture had come.
She saw the nails in your hands and feet,
as her heart ached for her son.

The soldiers and leaders mocked you.
They offered you sour wine.
"Save yourself," they laughed and shouted,
but you knew it wasn't your time.

The separation from your Father
was worse than physical pain.
You carried our load of sins.
Still on the cross you remained.

You died and were placed in a tomb
giving your followers much despair.
The third day freedom came.
Death could not keep you there.

Lord Jesus, we will always be grateful
that you came down from above.
A sacrifice we didn't deserve,
to show us your unending love.

## Lost Souls

The Trinity, we don't understand. We know that Jesus existed from the beginning. He said, "If you have seen me then you've seen the Father that is in me."

We are to have faith and trust in the Lord.

I often wonder how those living without the Lord make it through the day. Where do they turn when they're in need, or pain, or have lost a loved one.

God please help them, your lost sheep.

## *Christ Our Father*

Christ our Creator God
gave His human body for us.
In Him we are blessed.
In Him we should place our trust.

He heads His Body the Church.
He gives gifts to those He holds dear.
To each person, He gives talents.
He comforts those who have fear.

He helps the blind to see
and causes the lame to walk.
He opens ears to hear
and helps those mute, to talk.

Christ saves our souls.
He suffered and died for our sin.
He mends the broken hearted.
Spiritual battles, He helps us win.

He's a thoughtful, loving Father
who tenderly cares for His young.
He created all there is
and existed before all had begun.

# *God Bless America*

When the Twin Towers came done in New York by terrorists on 9/11/01, America was stunned. We couldn't believe that we had been attacked here at home. Our war with evil began. As we continue the battle in Iraq with the lose of many of our fine men and women fighting for freedom, we are united in our prayer for peace.

"God Bless America."

# *The Battle*

With thundering blasts, the battle raged.
Billowing smoke filled the sky.
Blazing fires burned with vengeance,
reflecting in each captive's eyes.

Silence echoed the countryside,
then another blast rocked the earth.
A mushroom cloud appeared.
Into flames, the target burst.

Sand storms wreaked their havoc.
Blinded, the men marched on.
Like masked bandits, they led their charge
as mortars fired shots till dawn.

Then daylight cast eerie shadows
over a blood drenched battlefield.
Cries were heard in the distance.
In defeat, the enemy did yield.

God heard each tormented soul
and cradled them with care.
He understood their suffering.
He knew, for He was there.

The war in Iraq started:

# *Lost*

We don't have to travel far to see a homeless person. We must find a way to help them.

A community shelter needs to be established for those who have lost their way. We never know, we might be entertaining an Angel.

When we are warm and cozy in our home, there are many without a coat.

May this be a reminder to do what Jesus would have us do. Love your neighbor as yourself. Our neighbor is not just the person next door.

Help us Lord to help others.

# *The Homeless*

They wander along life's highway
with no place to call their own.
Their bodies ache for rest,
a place to call their home.

Their faded misty eyes
stare blankly into space.
A gaunt and haggard look
is written on their face.

They trudge along this highway
with a companion called despair.
Their hope for a better day
is dashed by lack of care.

Do you see these helpless people,
or do you walk on by?
Is your heart filled with compassion
as you hear their lonely cry?

Your arms are the arms of God
to cradle those in pain.
The love you give to them
will also be your gain.

## *Bridle Your Tongue*

How many times have unkind words slipped from our tongue? It's hard to bridle your tongue. We think, "Oh if we just would have kept quiet." How many times have each of us had to eat our own words? They don't go down very well.

We must stay alert and stay in God's word. Our prayer should be to be more like Jesus.

As He stood before Pilot, He never said a word.

Help us please Father to bridle our tongue.

## *The Tongue*

Sometimes it spills out profanity
wounding all those that hear.
Its deadly poison, lethal,
like the thrust from a well aimed spear.

It can gallop out of control
as a stallion not yet broken.
Yet can lay silent in its bed
without a word being spoken.

What a strange member, the tongue,
as it pours out evil and good.
It's very hard to control
and doesn't do what it should.

Every animal, bird or fish,
man is able to train.
But the small independent tongue,
no human is able to tame.

Live a life of steady goodness.
Ask God for wisdom each day.
Always be peace loving and courteous
and be aware of what you say.

# *The Price of Freedom*

When we sit in our comfortable home or attend the church of our choice, do we take our freedom for granted.

Our forefathers planned for freedom as they wrote the Constitution. America was and is a place to seek freedom.

Our young men and women continue to fight for this cause.

God please bless our leaders and give them wisdom to make Godly decisions.

In God we trust.

# *United We Stand*

May the light of hope shine on
as terrorism crosses our shore.
May we rise to this challenge
and say, "We're not taking it anymore".

Our country was built on freedoms
that our forefathers planned long ago.
May we proudly raise our banner
and let peace be what we sow.

America weeps for her children
and mourns those she's lost.
May they not have died in vain.
May we remember freedom's cost.

Let's bridle all our wisdom.
Let's fight to stamp out fear.
Let's pray to God for help
as we mourn those we hold dear.

May love be our resolve.
May we reach out and hold hands.
Let's march together for America
and bravely take out stand.

# *God's Creation*

From my sunroom, I look out over the mountains. It is such an awesome sight. It's like a National Geographic panoramic view.
   How could anyone discount the majesty of our Creator God.
   When I see the tiniest little perfect flower at my feet, I praise the Lord.
   We must always be good stewards of His Creation

# *From My Window*

From my window I see God's creation.
Mist covered mountains arise.
Darkness is creeping into dawn,
right before my eyes.

I think of how God gathered the waters
and called the waters, seas.
He named the dry land, earth
and our Creator God was pleased.

He called forth all living things.
Stars appeared in the sky.
He placed the moon to govern the night.
Over day, the sun did preside.

From my window, I behold His creation
and all His expressions of love.
It's awesome to think of His Holiness
while He looks down on us from above.

## *Forgiveness*

Forgiveness is a godly decision, however it can be very hard to do. We say we forgive but unfortunately we don't forget.

We find it most difficult to forgive ourselves. We seem to have a ticker tape in our brain that keeps reminding us of whatever we've done.

The devil is alive and well and takes pleasure in condemning us.

We must ask for God's help, for he says if we don't forgive, we won't be forgiven and that includes not forgiving ourselves.

# *Turmoil*

Turmoil distress our soul,
when hurt by a very close friend.
His apology we say we accept,
but our heart's unable to mend.

We look at this person we loved
and remember the wrong he has done.
We wallow around in self pity
and are fooled that forgiveness has come.

Our nagging self-centered thoughts
are hard for us to give up.
We want to feel peace in our soul,
but bitterness brews ;in our cup

        "AND GOD SAID"

"Remember my loving Son
who died on the cross for you.
He prayed, Father forgive them,
for they know not what they do."

This lesson we all should learn
from Jesus our teacher and friend.
that forgiveness is a healing balm
for a broken heart needing to mend.

## *The Sin of Pride*

Dwelling on our imperfections and what others think of us is an example of the sin of pride.

    I lived many years without recognizing this sin and even now it creeps in when I don't realize it. Even making excuses why we didn't do something, is another way we open the door to prideful thoughts

    Lord, please forgive our sin of pride.

        Thank you.

## *Downward Path*

How glaring seem our imperfections
as we dwell on what people think.
So easy it is to lose perspective
as deeper into self we sink.

This path we walk at times
has no hurdles to get in our way.
The devil strolls along it
and that's where h wants you to stay.

He has helpers that'll pity you
and listen to your problems each day.
They falsely sooth your wounds
and don't stop and say, "Lets pray."

Beware of this well traveled path
and those people holding you down.
Read the word of God
where wisdom can be found.

## *Happiness*

Happiness is very hard to define. I heard a program one time where the speaker explained happiness as striving to accomplish something, but when the project was completed, happiness seemed to fade.

We cannot compare happiness with joy. Joy is a gift from God that we can share with others. The joy of feeling the presence of God within you is way beyond happiness.

# *Traveling to Happiness*

We travel the road toward happiness,
ever seeking contentment and peace.
When projects are completed,
we give a big sigh of relief.

Then tomorrow comes to reign
with new challenges we must face.
The peace of our yesterday,
reaps new problems in its place.

Where is the happiness we seek
as we fritter away our time?
Did we lose it in the shuffle
while life's problems wait in line?

What we have is just today.
Find joy in what you do.
Happiness will then fill your soul
and God will smile on you.

Psalms 28

# Choose Wisely

I remember talking to my children about making good decisions. I also reminded them about choosing their friends wisely.

Our reputation goes with us. We can only improve ourselves by the help of God.

We must pray and ask the Holy Spirit to teach us and pray for us. He is gentle and kind.

Our greatest resource is the Bible. Jesus teaches through His word as well as by example.

Fellowship with believers and covet their prayers for you.

# *Your Reputation*

Your reputation goes with you
and holds as a clinging vine.
Running gives no resolve
and truth will surface in time.

Your excuse to place blame,
like a beacon, exposes you.
Look with honest judgment
at reasons for what you do.

Study and improve yourself.
Be ready to face a new day.
Do your work as unto the Lord.
His reward will be added pay.

Cherish a good reputation.
Treat it with thought and prayer.
A clear conscience will be your mascot
and happiness is what you'll share.

## *Our Lost Children*

Where are we as a society, when we allow babies to be aborted. God knows the plan He had for their lives.

In China they have decided to allow only one child per family. They are finding out that their census is showing more male births than female. It seems mothers are having ultrasounds and aborting female babies.

Oh Father God, please help us to value human life and forgive our sins as a nation.

# *The Aborted Child*

Oh how I cried when you rejected me,
as I lay quiet in my bed.
I thought you loved me, mother mine,
but you tossed me aside instead.

What a strange world it must be
that doesn't protect its young.
If only they'd ask an innocent child,
what a wonderful world it could become.

Oh Father of all, I don't understand
how someone could treat me this way.
Wasn't I loved enough by them?
Why did I have to pay?

God looked at me with tear stained face,
and reached out His loving hand.
It was not only you that received no embrace
but also the Savior of man.

## A Mother's Loss

While working as a psychiatric nurse, I had a patient that had gotten pregnant. She heard many pros and cons about whether to have an abortion or not. I talked to her at length about having her baby and placing it up for adoption.

I came back to work one day and discovered she did have an abortion. Her guilt and sadness was almost more than she could bear.

How God must weep for all the aborted babies.

## Abortion — "A Mother's Loss"

They didn't tell me I'd hear him cry,
while peace struggles in my soul.

They didn't tell me my empty womb,
would weep bloody tears to be full.

They didn't tell me the heartache I'd feel,
while dealing with my guilt and shame.

They didn't tell me how lost I would be
as I drown in a sea of such pain.

Can you help me, oh God, as I live with my loss,
and forgive all the wrong I have done?

The foot of the cross is the answer, my child.
That's where the battle was won.

978-0-595-43475-6
0-595-43475-4